I Lost My Blackberry
Down the Toilet

I Lost My Blackberry Down the Toilet

And Other Generational Challenges In the Workplace

Steven M. Friedman

iUniverse, Inc.

New York Lincoln Shanghai

I Lost My Blackberry Down the Toilet
And Other Generational Challenges In the Workplace

iUniverse books may be ordered through booksellers or by contacting:

iUniverse
2021 Pine Lake Road, Suite 100
Lincoln, NE 68512
www.iuniverse.com
1-800-Authors (1-800-288-4677)

ISBN-13: 978-0-595-40129-1 (pbk)
ISBN-13: 978-0-595-84509-5 (ebk)
ISBN-10: 0-595-40129-5 (pbk)
ISBN-10: 0-595-84509-6 (ebk)

Printed in the United States of America

CONTENTS

▼

Foreword

Recently I was on a vacation. As a consultant with clients all over the country, I need to be available and in-touch all the time. In a typical week 1,000 emails seem almost quiet, so while on a cruise taking a day trip to Costa Rica, I decided to take my remote technology with me. If I didn't want to spend the bulk of my time walking back and forth to the Internet café, I needed to have my Blackberry.

Fortunately, I was able to use my Blackberry on the shore of Costa Rica. Lucky me and my need to be connected! Onto the tour bus I marched, Blackberry fastened to the belt on my shorts, wired with technology, and wired with a few cups of coffee. I settled into my seat to enjoy the day. It didn't take long for my Baby Boomer bladder to kick-in, but with a lavatory in the bus, I was safe. I traipsed to the rear of the bus, opened the lavatory door, and felt lucky for the convenient location.

The roads in Costa Rica are not like the roads in the states. There are ruts and bumps and narrow shoulders. As I stood balancing myself in the bathroom, the bus hit a sudden bump. I was jostled, and out of my holster...flew the Blackberry—down the trap door in the toilet.

My life was flying before my eyes.

However, this was not the first time. Several years ago, I was on a plane—a daily occurrence. Again, it was an early morning flight, and with too much coffee imbibed, I unhooked my seat belt and headed to the lavatory. Turbulence shook the plane, and off flew my Blackberry down the chute.

This was not how my father vacationed or traveled on business! The Traditionalists way of going on vacation was to log off for a period of time and let the office buzz along without you. There were no cell phones, no email, and no instant communication that allowed you to work while you played. Boomers were no different. We went off to commune with ourselves and to get in touch with our inner person. We paid no heed to life back at the office. After all, that was the point of our vacations—to separate ourselves from work, not to connect. But the emerging generations have changed all that. The way we used to be just does not exist anymore.

So why this book?

Losing that Blackberry sent me a signal. Something has really changed. What occurred to me was that new generations in the workplace are creating challenges we have never before encountered. The new generations come with different expectations, different goals, and different approaches to how they view their work life. We clearly need to understand the "whys and hows" of such changes so we can develop the skills we need at each generational level to cope.

Having been a consultant to the real estate industry for 17 years it becomes clear that there are business models that are problematic to a multiple generational hiring model. The Real estate industry in particular battles these generational issues, with many traditionalist based business models impacting the ability to merge the generations in a productive peaceful co-existence.

Leadership often does not sense the impact, and must address these issues soon, or the consequences could be severe.

As the book progresses it is important to the reader to envision how one industry is not coping well with generational change, why the generations really do have different business needs, and how the options may actually enhance an important business sector.

WHY STUDY THE GENERATIONS?

Remember the paper menus in Chinese restaurants with the twelve animals of the zodiac? According to the Chinese zodiac, every person born in a particular year shared similar personality traits represented by a certain animal. If you were born in 1960, for example, you are a rat—generous and charming but quick-tempered and critical. How could the Chinese zodiac claim that sharing the same birth year suggested an entire group of people possessed the same defining characteristics? The arrival of steamed dumplings usually diverted my curiosity and droplets of soy sauce blurred the rat into the dragon.

Many years later, my wonder resurfaced as I began to observe the interplay of a multi-generation workplace. I soon recognized that sharing the same birth year did influence personality and behavior in ways that directly affected the success and growth of organizations. Open the door to thinking like a "generational sleuth" and you begin to appreciate why one group of people occupying the same demographic space in time share so many of the same values, characteristics, and patterns of behavior.

For the first time in American history, four generations inhabit the workplace creating a new diversity that is transforming the real estate industry. Historically, workplace diversity revolved around women, minorities, and lifestyle choices, but now a new diversity dominates the workforce. The convergence of four generations, each with its own vision of how the world works, necessitates a new model for attracting and retaining the most talented people to your organization. To understand the diverse generations in your organization, you must see the world through their eyes and recognize how their "generational lenses" influence how they interact with clients, colleagues, and management. These lenses determine perceptions of fairness and equality within the workplace, and they create the foundation for organizational success or failure. Organizations that hope to attract, manage, and retain the four generations must endeavor to understand who these generations are and what makes them tick.

Each generation comes of age with a shared history defined by key conditions and reference points. This historical identity is determined more by sociological and psychological factors than simply the year you were born. No hard and fast rules claim which generation you belong to—dates are approximate and debatable; it is the lens through which you view the world that more aptly identifies your generational label. While many factors contribute to personality and disposition, the extent that you connect with the people, places, things, and events of a particular generation influences who you are and how you see the world. While your 1963 birth year may mark you as a Baby Boomer, the formative experiences that shaped your first fifteen years of life might more accurately define you as a Generation Xer.

The four generations in our workplace today:

- Traditionalists   (Born between 1940–1945: about seventy-five million)

- Baby Boomers   (Born between 1946–1964: about eighty million)

- Generation X   (Born between 1965–1980: about forty-six million)

- Millennials   (Born after 1980: about seventy-six million)

Generational differences effect interpersonal relationships and customer service relationships. They affect who is attracted to your organization and why. They affect your recruiting practices and your management practices. Ultimately, how you understand generational diversity affects your productivity and success as talented people choose to remain with your organization or exit through the revolving door.

This milieu of population is not without interaction, yet the interaction and understanding of unique business goals is not frequently clear between the groups. Too many leaders in the industry are confused by the demands of the other generations in their midst, to the point of diminished interest from younger generations in the Real Estate industry as a whole.

Recently noted publications including the "Wall Street Journal" have devalued the appealing nature of Real Estate as an industry of choice for business school graduates.

For a business segment so critical to the economy this is not a position that should be acceptable.

A typical office story:

Jane is the manager of a large sales staff. There are 50+ individuals that sell real estate out of her office. By and large, the population of her team falls into two groups: most are either Traditionalists or Boomers. They have all sold real estate for some time and although they are embracing the technological changes that the workplace requires, it is not without real resistance. The Traditionalists believe you have to see a house to sell it or buy it, and because they have done it the same way for so long, new methods unsettle them. The thought of a being in constant communication with clients and customers is a battle, and the need for a tool like a PDA is unfathomable.

The Traditionalists fail to address their need to change. As they shun the real conversations, they adopt the attitude that they have done things their way for so long, changing to approach things in a new way seems odd and uncomfortable. They trust their instincts, which are rooted in the past, and continue to do business with tried and true methods. Many in this group are not educated at advanced levels and have learned the hard way by using street smarts to guide their successes.

This group has in many cases come into the technology age kicking and screaming. It was not too long ago that they were intimidated by the idea of leaving messages on voice mail, or to open air on an answering machine. Only recently have they accepted the necessity of using a cell phone.

In the office team, none of the team downloads music, and they would hardly consider making a purchase online. They avoid the concept of virtual tours and use email only as a last resort.

The boomer group is a bit more willing to embrace technology, as they run the gamut from being highly tech savvy to showing resistance and inertia.

Four new agents have joined this office in the recent month: a Traditionalist, a Boomer, a Generation Xer, and a Millennial. The Traditionalist agent has decided that selling real estate might be a good career option for her retirement. She can do this as she pleases, and no one will hold her accountable to the performance and pressure she had in her previous career. She wants the freedom to work by her own standards and her own timetable. She wants lots and lots of hands-on training, and she is taking time to study the resources she needs to prepare herself.

The Boomer agent is anxious to learn but wants to be given some bold headlines about how to get things done and then to be left alone to either make it or not. Training seems to be of little interest unless it is in brief, short snippets. The Boomer is used to being thrown-in and surviving, and feels she needs just enough information to get her going without the details that coherent, comprehensive training can provide.

Before the Generation Xer agent even walked through the office door, she had already been on the company intranet site, clicked onto the training links, and completed two on-line classes that the organization offered. She researched several blogs for details on how some agents are reaching their clients, but she is frustrated that the training is not downloadable by pod cast. She is surprised there are not any FAQ's to guide her on how to get things done quickly, and she is frustrated that her questions about marketing and business can only be done face to face with her manager. Her overall opinion is that the learning pace is too slow and she fears the company may lack the cutting edge technology she is accustomed to.

The Millennial agent feels the office leadership looks down on her because of her age. She has a high need for coaching and communication, but she frequently feels patronized as being too young to have valid experiences. She is already planning to leave the organization as she is not about to wait around "to pay her dues" simply because she is a novice in business, particularly when she is more tech savvy than her manager.

Business has become a bit difficult as the prior market that agents had been experiencing is not happening now. The manager of the office that experienced the last slow market 12 years ago has forgotten how to guide agents to do business in a tough market. In fact the mangers expertise in transaction management rather than on business development is echoing negative feelings among the agents group. The internet demands on the business have certainly created angst among the team. The younger population wants concrete business development recipes the more senior group hesitates to even connect. The manager as a result is caught in a business environment where no one is being made happy or guided appropriately.

Unfortunately this is a far too familiar scene today. The Manager is frustrated, as she does not know the strategies she needs to have in place to reach these four new and very different affiliates. The manager's personal style is more suited to the Traditionalists, although she can identify and relate to the needs of her Boomers. She is, however, not at all tuned into the trends that drive the two younger generations, and because of this, she risks failing to recognize their value and potential productivity. The result is she could have a terrible retention dilemma as the managers of a newer younger generation of agents refuse to connect with this group. Furthermore, the senior generational groups are not getting what they need either as they are not truly open to deep business coaching. As a result a retention dilemma of major proportions occurs, as agents fail to do business.

This book is designed to provide the reader with a guideline as to why the generations react in their own unique and different way and how **solid leadership** can reach them all on their own terms. Read on...

Defining The Generations: Who Are They?

Traditionalists
Born between 1900–1945

Sometimes referred to as the Silent Generation or the GI generation, Traditionalists encompass two generations who share similar values and characteristics. Born between 1900–1945, and sandwiched between the two world wars, this generation is notable for their patriotism and loyalty. As children of the Great Depression and the New Deal, Traditionalists learned to work diligently not just for success, but for survival. War and instability necessitated sacrifice, and they knew what life was like living without. Their upbringing taught them to put their individual needs aside to focus on the greater needs of the whole. Shaped by the lean years of their youth, they conscientiously saved money, and to this day prefer using cash in lieu of credit. "A penny saved is a penny earned" and "Save for a rainy day" reflect their history and their conservative spending styles.

By and large this was a generation that was born from immigrants. They lived in clustered homogeneous areas where the ethnicity was often similar. These people fled the old country, and what they had in America in this era was a great improvement, even if they were not always well off financially.

This generation was generally not well educated and the lack of formal advanced education was often seen as a challenge that could limit their potential. As there was so much hope for a strong, solid future, this generation often tolerated lifestyle choices that were in many ways not satisfying, while dreaming to build a future for their families.

Traditionalists generally spent their lives in one career and with one organization. If they had a good job that enabled them to provide for their families, they remained regardless of whether the work relationship was fulfilling or not. They paid their dues and worked hard to move up the career ladder. Traditionalists are dubious of the promotional fluidity and career hopping younger generations enjoy today. They view retirement as a reward for the many years devoted to their companies.

Social order and conformity guide how Traditionalists interact and communicate within the organization. Their respect for authority and desire to maintain the status quo inhibit them from challenging decisions made by leadership. More than fifty percent of the men in this generation are veterans, and their military experiences instilled a faith in top-down approaches of command that continue to influence the structure of organizational growth to this day.

Traditionalists embrace old myths of business believing only those with experience in the real estate industry understand what is really going on. They prefer organizations that are uniform and consistent in style, and they favor formal work environments in terms of dress, communication, and business structures.

This generation has a deep faith in institutions and their implied legacy. They watched as organizations, religious institutions, the government, and the military joined together to win wars, fight poverty, and stabilize America. Their loyalty remains and is unmatched by the generations that followed.

Defining Moments and People

- The Great Depression

- The GI Bill

- The New Deal

- World War II

- The death of Franklin Delano Roosevelt

- Radio and movies

Defining Characteristics

- Loyal

- Patriotic

- Dutiful

- Conforming

- Conservative

- Hardworking

- Respect authority

- Faith in institutions

- Conscientious with money

- Desire consistency, uniformity, and formality

A Story of a classic Traditionalist

Mary is a Traditionalist. She has worked in the company selling for 25 years and can't imagine working for anyone else. Once upon a time she was a military wife and was used to moving every few years. Her husband retired form service, took a corporate job and encouraged her to go into the real Estate business because she was so good with people. Her educational background does not truly exist as she married at 19. She is in her late sixties and is looking forward to retiring in the next three years. She grew up during World War II and remembers well her father's return from the war with an injury, and how he worked relentlessly to regain his health. She grew up in Detroit on a street where there was one ethnicity—hers. She was used to being around people who were exactly like her, and saw how the few people in her neighborhood who were different were mistrusted. Being in a military household she had to quickly adapt to different parts of the world. She was adept at creating peer groups but, like many military wives, did not have the formal education. She learned by doing and adapting.

Working was far from her mind growing up in the late forties and fifties, as she imagined herself playing Mah Jong and tennis and taking care of a family. In her generation everyone knew husbands worked—wives didn't. the military background and frequent moves never allowed her to truly develop a career. Careers with choices were not truly open to her. She sat nicely by her husbands side.

In 1964, things began to change: Her husband left the military, had serious business problems, and was downsized twice. So to help her family, she went to work and began her career as a real estate agent. She built her business person-to-person, meeting the ladies she played tennis with and selling them their homes. She was unstoppable, determined that if she just kept at it, nothing would get in her way. Her military wife background gave her great empathy for loneliness as people relocated and she became a relocation expert.

She succeeded, and her organization rewarded her with leads and referrals because she could handle them and turn those leads into revenue.

She respected her organization and was thrilled to be a part of its dynamic growth. She was widely recognized by its leaders as a top producer. Because she had suffered huge business challenges through her husband, she was emphatic about saving and investing money. She just did it all the same, continually. That was until now.

Suddenly she was feeling like an antiquated relic. It happened so fast, she couldn't quite put her finger on when the changes began to affect her status. Her way of doing business was vanishing and she was feeling hard pressed to stay in the business at all.

She has stropped receiving referrals as the new relocating buyers have internet business demands that she has not subscribed to. They have a communication need that the military wives of the past, many of whom were her customer's just did not need. She subscribed to a philosophy that required people to see a house to buy it. The concept of having a virtual tour to sell a house is just in her mind silly.

As a result this year her business is off 36%. Her manager has tried to boost her up by telling her what a great agent, but it isn't working. The phrase, "you know what to do" which has worked in the past, is falling flat. Knowing what to do is not a clear model, and the way she has operated these last years seems to have vanished. She is hiding in a traditionalist zone unwilling to change—and worse yet, the leadership she requires is full of clichés about how to change.

Exercise for Discussion:

In the above story how might you go about shifting the result if you were the leadership here?

BABY BOOMERS
Born 1946–1964

The Baby Boomer generation began when World War II ended and veterans returned home to their wives. It was the largest generation ever born in America at one time. In some areas, hospitals were so overcrowded with mothers ready to give birth beds lined hallways to accommodate all the mothers in labor. Dr. Spock entered the scene in 1946 with his first edition of the child-rearing bible, *Baby and Childcare.* He advised parents to give lots of love and attention to their children and Traditionalists listened. While some critics blamed Dr. Spock for creating an overly permissive parenting style, Boomers grew up highly social, optimistic, and ready to change the world.

Boomers were raised teeming with opportunities that their parents never had the luxury to enjoy. The postwar economy was a good time for families; jobs were plentiful, production of consumer goods proliferated, and the promise of a quality education for everyone infused the American spirit. The self-sacrifice necessary during wartime and the Depression had ended.

Unaffected by the struggles of the Traditionalists before them, Boomers made it their personal mission to transform the cultural and political face of America. In contrast to their "silent" parents, optimistic Boomers loudly vocalized their dissatisfaction with the status quo. They were the "me" generation, anti-establishment to the core, quick to challenge authority, and dedicated to remaking the ideals of their parents. Boomers successfully pushed for change in civil rights, reproductive rights, women's rights, and human rights. This was the first generation of women to seek fulfilling careers as an alternative to staying home to raise kids. They affirmed non-traditional relationships and acknowledged divorce as an acceptable relationship alternative. Experience taught them that change was possible and they carried this optimism into their adulthood.

Driven by their successes, the work force became more diversified which paved the way for women to brake through the glass ceilings of corporate America. The real estate industry was one of the first to recognize that women outperformed their male counterparts in dramatic ways. The Boomers' legacy of acceptance broke down dated practices in which brokers requested husband/wife interviews to verify the spouse supported the candidate.

Boomers were the first generation to grow up with TV. In 1956, American homes claimed four million TV sets; by 1960 that number had jumped to 50 million. The violent images of race riots, anti-war demonstrations, and political assassinations unveiled the inequalities and social unrest in America. For the first time, an entire generation experienced shared images of significant political events leading them to question deeply the values they were raised with.

Defined by the medium of TV, Boomers were the focus of every major consumer product for the past twenty-five years. When the first mall opened in 1956, shopping changed forever. Revolving charge cards were invented for the sheer consumerisms of this generation with their buy now pay later spending style. Boomers dominated every new fad and trend. From Levi's to bell-bottoms and mood rings to bandanas—whatever they latched onto became the next hot item. They grew up brand conscious, materialistic, and status focused.

The sheer number of Boomers vying for the best schools, the best jobs, and the best resources meant this generation had to develop a fierce competitive spirit if they were to get what they wanted. They prize their careers and tend to be workaholics. Unlike the Traditionalists who conscientiously saved money, Boomers choose to spend what they have. It is widely recognized that this group has mortgaged their future.

Their strong work ethic supports their spending habits and enables them to enjoy a standard of living higher than that of their parents, their grandparents, and their great-grandparents. This group was educated to achieve what the previous generations had not.

As they slowly come to terms with the reality of their age, they are beginning to direct their thinking inward realizing there is more to life than working constantly, accumulating possessions, and accruing debt.

This generation is so consumption oriented that new industries are emerging continually to cater top the needs of the aging Boomer. The Boomer does not see themselves retiring in their sixties and does not see the end of a career but rather the re-invention and continuance of work into their 70's. After all 60 is the new 40!

Defining Moments and People

- Civil Rights Movement

- Assassination of John F. Kennedy

- The death of Marilyn Monroe

- Vietnam War

- Public protests

- "Beatles and the English Invasion"

- Woodstock

- The Cold War

- Watergate

Defining Characteristics

- Competitive

- Optimistic

- Anti-establishment

- Love/hate relationship with authority

- Workaholics

- Media driven

- Team workers

- Relationships revolve around personal gratification

- Consumption focused

- Political at work

- Status focused

A Boomer's challenge:

Raised in the sixties, Sue grew up expecting to go to college and to get a degree. She was far more directed than the women of even ten years earlier; she was not simply going to college to find a husband, she wanted a career.

As a college student in the late sixties, Sue was politically active and demonstrated for the right to equal treatment by employers. She even burned her bra at a rally.

With an MBA in hand, Sue dove head first into the business world. While studying for her degree she was an oddity a woman in a mans' world. Yet, she was going to have it all. She loved the competitive nature of achieving in a man's world and wasn't afraid to go head to head with her male bosses to attain her goals. She quickly devel-

oped a reputation for being an overachiever and often outworked her male counter-parts.

As Sue's career grew, so did her family. But that didn't stop her. She would leave the house, drop the kids off at daycare, pick them up at the end of the day, stop for dinner at McDonalds (which they ate in the car), and all the while continue to drive herself up the corporate ladder.

She worked long hours and often imposed upon her parents to watch the kids while she toiled in her office on the weekends. Her husband was no help, as he too was an avid workaholic, and as their careers grew, they grew apart.

Then, a choice had to be made. Sue was offered a job, but out of state. Sue's husband had a job here but was not achieving the same success that Sue had achieved. So, the decision was whose career would take priority over the other. They decided to relocate for Sue's career and the husband became a trailing spouse. His career never again reached the pinnacle.

After several years they divorce, and in 1989 life changed dramatically. Sue's company was downsized. After all of her sacrifices, she lost her job. She contributed over 80% of the family income, was now divorced and was faced with a horrendous life challenge—how to be a working single Mom and provide for her children. Even more, she had to pay the husband alimony!

Knowing she could sell and communicate well with men in a workplace she examined her strengths. To re-evaluate her career she sought guidance and introspection.

Sue decided she would sell real estate. She knew the president of a local company and gave him a call. He told her she would be terrific, and she was. Sue was a "killer". Nothing could stop her. She prospected on the phone with diligence, held open houses continually and grabbed every client she could as she also invested herself.

Year after year she fiercely beat out the competition and was recognized for her achievements at many award dinners and banquets. She reveled in the public recognition her company bestowed upon her. These awards always spurred her on to greater achievements.

In 2004 her company was sold. The old president was no longer around to recognize her achievements. She suddenly felt that even with her success, she was undervalued. She could no longer count on the power base that had so long rooted for her. She felt lost and adrift even though her true business surroundings had not changed. She was lost at sea, unsure if she'd ever regain her former status.

Then her manager was fired because of office consolidation and the loving praise was gone too. Her power base had shrunk to zero. She was just a name in a big environment, still receiving recognition, but not feeling secure in what now was an unfamiliar environment.

She feels lost .

Exercise:

As Sues situation is examined what would work well to drive her career for-ward if you were her leader.

GENERATION X

Generation X, poised to fill the void left by the potential of retiring Boomers and Traditionalists, is probably the most misunderstood and misjudged generation in the workforce today.

Born between 1965–1980, Generation X is only a little more than half the size of the Boomers before them and the Millennials that follow. While older generations may wrestle with the elusive Xer personality, understanding the environment that created Generation X sheds light on who they are and what makes them tick.

Generation X was the most under-supervised generation in America's history. During Xers birth years, two trends combined to create a generation of latch key kids: The divorce rate tripled resulting in single, working mothers raising their children, and dual income households replaced the stay-at-home moms from the generation before.

With house keys strung around their necks, Generation Xers came home from school to empty homes where they managed their own homework, cooked their own meals, and passed the time watching TV or playing Atari. These kids did not go outside to play—they occupied themselves with unstructured activities that served as time fillers at home. Independent and resourceful, Xers grew up learning to care for themselves. They were told go home put something in the Microwave, watch a video in the VCR, I'll pick you up and we'll go to McDonalds for dinner and then you will do your homework while Mom (or dad) gets some work done at home.

In many cases, these kids became confidants for their parents who were having divorce issues and often learned of life challenges well before their time. They learned adult issues that they were truly not ready to absorb and as a result had to face life issues that they just were ill prepared to handle. The AIDS crisis led to frank discussions about sexual issues at a very young age that were never before discussed at this age level.

As Xers experienced the breakdown of the nuclear family, they also witnessed the breakdown of corporate institutions. They watched their parents, whose lives revolved around work, fall victim to corporate readjusting and organizational downsizing. This imprinted itself on the Xer's psyche, creating a distrust of institutions and skepticism for career relationships that promised longevity and loyalty.

They became devout realists, recognizing that personal success was self-won. They truly were aware that they had to achieve on their own. Unlike their parents, whose careers revolved around a single organization; this generation would not put all their eggs in one basket at the cost of missing out on family experiences. Prioritization and balance became the guide for Xers' lives.

The concept of time forever changed under Generation X so that whatever could not arrive instantly was not worth having. Cell phones and personal computers made communication and information instant, fast food restaurants and microwaves made mealtime instant, and ATMs spout out money—instantly. Wait time and patience shrunk as every aspect of life offered the opportunity for rapid response. Waiting in a line for anything was not a situation this group handled well This altered sense of time becomes glaring in the workplace as older generations often lament the lack of patience and forbearance Xers exhibit.

Generation X was the first generation to grow up driven by technology. The worldwide web afforded quick and current access to information and a global network, and technology that was less than cutting edge seemed archaic to them. Their vision of diversity and multi-culturalism became vastly different than the generations before them, partly because of their exposure to an on-line global community. While Xers drove the technology boom, they were most affected emotionally and financially by the bursting of the dot.com bubble, which further fueled their cynicism in the stability of organizations.

Xers' desire for freedom and balance frustrate older generations. Generation Xers are masters at compartmentalizing business and pleasure. They work to live, refusing to put in the same long hours their parents did at the expense of missing out on the important moments in their children's lives. Business is business and pleasure is pleasure and if the two are to meet, it's on Xer's terms, not management's.

The self-reliant and self-motivated nature of Generation X explains why they have churned out the largest percentage of entrepreneurs this country has ever known. Their devotion to personal success, trusting in their own devices, and refusing to acknowledge the status quo propel this phenomenon and testify to the fact that Xers may be hard to define but not hard to motivate.

This generation also benefited from the tech boom. They possess skills that were needed, but not truly understood by the previous senior generations. In fact their knowledge was almost voodoo like too many. They carved out niches in companies where tech needs exceeded knowledge. They were unduly compensated based upon this specific knowledge trading income dollars for stock options, making them more money than their parents at a young age. The companies they joined were IPO's and the instant 20–30 something millionaires were created without the traditional career stair step career paths.

This group then focused on different values: technology use and application could be the road to riches. Once again the instant "I don't have to wait" mentality played itself out. The video game generation did not have to proceed down the traditional roads to achieve success. Instant gratification was now the rule.

This generation also became cynical as the options they accepted as salary became worthless as the Tech bubble crashed in the late 90's. Once again they were caught by circumstances they could not control. In addition these Tech savvy people were allowed to work in non-disciplined atmospheres, some equating work clothes to jeans and a t-shirt rather than a suit and tie. The result being that normal corporate environments seemed far too constrained for their free wheeling styles.

The Real Estate industry in particular has experienced many Gen X challenges. First the industry was never tech focused as the population assumes that one would need to see houses to buy them. The data collected by real estate management was never tech focused so there was a challenge of how to drive and manage this population. Although inventory data was often controlled by the industry it has become increasingly more available at the "demand" of internet savvy population's causing overt conflict. The Gen X demands on information requires ready access and the industry has only recently become aware of what that means.

The Gen X consumer facing the industry is far too self reliant to allow data about the industry to be sheltered and held back. Gen X has done more to challenge this industry than many others. Their need to control information and seek it at will are seen as antagonizing the traditionalist business model.

Defining Moments and People

The reality is generation X has few defining moments. The closest they come is the Gulf War where they forged a "kick your butt" attitude that the brief encounter demonstrated.

- Rise of Aids

- The Gulf War

- War on Drugs

- Crack cocaine

- The challenger Disaster

- Music videos

- Cable television

- CNN

Defining Characteristics

- Freedom

- Balance

- Autonomy

- Skeptical

- Distrustful of relationships

- Technologically savvy

- Individualistic

- Unimpressed by authority

- Status symbols fall flat

- "Sex and the City" is mainstream viewing and mass entertainment

Managing Ms. Cynical

Madison is 34 and just newly married. Fresh out of college, she had a top job in a PR firm that had a contract for a major tech company. She shifted her career from PR to tech support by creating interactive FAQ's (frequently asked questions) for her client. Madison and her husband lived together for a number of years before getting married, often commuting from city to city while they were both developing their careers. She was always on the go and decided to build her career first, and then think about family. There was no pressure to wed and she loved the freedom that high earnings gave her.

Madison realized she has created many portable experiences and is now considering real estate as a new career option. The big career has happened and she now believes she has maxed out the learning what most companies can provide. She is bored, recog-

nizing that her next move upwards is years away and feels unchallenged sitting around waiting for the boomer boss she has to retire.

She has researched career options inside her organization and is not looking to relocate to jump start her career and propel it forward as her parents might have.

In addition she has been telecommuting two days a week, logging into the company network from home. She is used to accessing the Instant Message network from where ever she is at the moment, getting in touch with people quickly via the internet and responds quickly. She believes face-to-face meetings are a waste of time and slows down work-flow.

Her Boomer Boss does not understand the telecommute style Madison prefers. The boss who was a Mom with three kids who worked 80 hours a week to get to her lofty position does not understand why Madison is so willing to ignore long hours in the office with politically recognized meeting and lunches to move her career forward. In her marketing position she has learned contact strategies that can move her forward. She understands how to reach a consumer via the Internet in specific terms and understands how to build flexibility into her environment. She is well educated, achievement oriented, and confident in her ability to build her next career.

When she resigns, her boss just doesn't get it and the exit interview becomes a diatribe on how as a woman achieves a top career. She says that Madison is failing women who worked so hard to achieve the status she now seeks. She should be ready to sacrifice to get ahead.

Selecting the organization to join was an interesting challenge for Madison. She emailed multiple managers for interviews and not even one responded. She found that they would only return phone calls. She wondered why they even had web sites if they did not understand they were contact points.

The managers she interviewed often led long dialogues about their companies and did not truly interview her to discover how she might impact the business, learn what her strategies might be, or understand how she envisioned driving a business. Madison was truly frustrated as the interviews were all selling sessions. Missing were the specific business recipes and tools that would make each organization unique. Managers continually positioned traditionalist style activities to get started. Madison does not want to sit in classrooms for hours on end to learn how to do business. She is looking for downloadable support and the ability to resource on her own, and she expects to drive her business with a flexible, nontraditional schedule.

The industry looked oddly out of touch. She noticed that there were not many of her peers in the offices she was interviewing. The office environments seemed very "clubby" and involved in archaic business strategy.

Ultimately she found one different organization that talked of business re-invention, peer access and strategy that sounded unique from the others.

Madison is inventing ways to do business daily. She has a blog that she uses to guide people to what is going on in the business, and she has podcast that she created to promote herself. Her manager encourages her to attend several traditional training classes where she spends excessive time championing the history of the company and how that history translates to assets for the agent. The company has a focused coaching program and is capable of showing her how to capture her peer group as buyers and sellers. In fact, Madison is delighted that her manager can truly demonstrate the success recipes of their brand and what make their systems unique. In fact Madison relishes in the directness of the tools and support she is receiving and the specific guidance to use key resources to build her business

MILLENNIALS
Born 1980 on......

Highly educated and achievement oriented, Millennials share more similarities with Boomers and Traditionalists than with their neighbor, Generation X. They are optimistic and confident, and with their great numbers, they will find themselves circumventing the corporate ladder to supplement the management gap left by aging Traditionalists and Boomers.

This generation does not see marriage in their twenties as a requirement. In fact the twenties is often recognized and an extended adolescence where growth and development out paces adult expectations.

Millennials truly grew up at time unlike any other. Technology dominates their life. Instant information, global communication, and unlimited options are their birthright. They never knew life without a remote in hand and less than a dozen channels to choose from. They never had to rely solely on the library when it came time to do research. And they never experienced what it was like to be out of reach because a pay phone was not nearby. A boomer icon—Paul Newman is recognized by Millennials as a salad dressing king not an actor.

Millennials were raised with fast paced lifestyles and tightly managed schedules. Unlike Boomers, who played with neighborhood friends after school, and Xers, who came home to their TVs and video games, Millennials began the second part of their day when the three o'clock bell rang. Parents charted an itinerary of extra-curricular activities to assure their child's well-rounded development: soccer, piano lessons, karate, cheerleading, foreign language, tutoring, and the list goes on.

Highly structured schedules left little free time, and Millennials learned to take advantage of any unfilled minute. Younger children worked on homework in the car between school and soccer, while older children finished homework with instant messaging, text messaging, and music playing in the background. The ability to filter massive amounts of stimulation at any given moment turned Millennials into adept multi-taskers, an asset they bring to the workplace.

Millennials grew up at a time when America could no longer rely on the safety of public spaces. The Oklahoma City bombing introduced homegrown terrorism, and Columbine, and other school shootings, permanently altered the assumption that school was an inherently safe place. The repertoire of normal school practices soon came to include lock-down drills and weapon searches. September 11, cemented the new world Millennials inherited, yet rather than responding with fear and hopelessness, a deepening patriotic spirit emerged. Yet this group is widel;y disillusioned as they have seen safe haens disappear as well as innocence in child hood vanish.

Diversity and multiculturalism infuse the Millennials's life. The influx of a new immigrant wave of often illegal immigrants will bring this generation to a crisis of greater proportion. The concept of immigration is a battle looming and could become in their future the civil rites issues of the 1960s.

Raised with "Character Counts" in the classroom, Millennials grew up volunteering and dedicating numerous hours to community service. They are strong advocates of giving back to the community and are attracted to organizations whose vision statements inspire a better world. Their honesty and integrity frame their goals for the future and have led Howe and Strauss in *Millennials Rising* to predict they will be America's next great generation.

Defining Moments and People

- Columbine

- Oklahoma City bombing

- 9/11

- Princess Diana's death

- Play Station, Xbox, and hand held video games

- Computers, Internet, cell phones

Defining Characteristics

- Patriotic

- Achievement oriented

- Community minded

- Collaborative

- Diverse

- Flexible

- Integrity

- Technologically driven

- Multitaskers

A Millennial Story

Brittany has just finished an MBA program at a major university. She is accustomed to using Instant Messaging to communicate with her professors during classes, as well as downloading their lectures to her MP3 player. She expects the same kind of technology and ease of communication to follow her into her career. Her desire to sell Real Estate is piqued because of the recent boom the industry has presented.

Brittany has been tracking property on the Internet and has become an inventory expert by using virtual tour technology to inspect and learn about properties online.

When she interviews at several offices her informal style and approach to the business sends chills through the managers. She is so casual and so technologically driven that she almost frightens her interviewer. Managers seem to patronize her lack of experience in the traditional sense, yet she has knowledge and background that many of her office group cannot grasp. Her frustration with the workplace dynamic is leading her to believe this is not the business for her.

Yet she has a real sense of listening to those that have been doing this for years. She has formed collaboration with a Traditionalist agent n the office who has limited tech skills and the two are teaching each other strategies they can each use. Brittany is learning the tools of the trade willingly from and expert whjile she also is teaching the expert how to use technology to drive her business. She introduced Zillow.com to her mentor with ease and is demonstrating the power of the web. She is far more willing to learn from those around her than Madison her office mate who is just to into her swelf to reach beyond her personal; walls seeking solutions.

CONFLICT ZONES

What happens when the gap between the generations becomes a quagmire of competing interests in the workplace? Because each generation has its own personality, its own messages that motivate, and its own workplace behaviors, certain actions are consistently misunderstood and become breeding grounds for performance and productivity challenges. When left unchecked, these differences create prime zones for potential conflict. Conflict zones revolve around the most basic differences in each generation's values and perceptions, and they are recognizable by the conversations you hear within the organization.

Following are some of the typical dialogues you might hear that reflect conflict zones:

- "They have no work ethic. They are a bunch of slackers."

Generation Xers are not focused on a nine-to-five life style. In the real estate industry, this group may be content to work at home on their computes at 9:00 p.m. and then present their contracts at a Starbucks. This is not the traditional approach of Boomers and Traditionalists, which leads to the perception that Xers are slackers. In reality Xers simply get their work done in a different time and space.

In the real estate industry specifically always known for a loose schedule environment this becomes particularly problematic. Most Traditionalist and Boomer agents do not set disciplined schedules yet they work odd hours and find themselves out at odd hours presenting contracts and showing property.

The Gen X agent will avoid the late hours will set boundaries of when they will and will not work and at the same time appears to be lazy to their senior peer groups. In fact it is not unusual to see the Gen X'er avoid the office to sit and work in the nearby Starbucks, a work environment the older groups do not recognize. The result is that the Gen X'er sees time and work spaces differently, creating the undue impression they are lazy.

It is also not unusual for the Gen X'er to have their Blackberry with them responding to communication needs instantly as well as shutting them off when they need to create family and personal time. The Gen X'er truly uses time to their advantage and typically does not have the overwhelmed feelings that the senior groups have by the aggressive communication demands they have from clients.

The Gen X'er will go to their child's soccer game at three but at midnight may be on their computer at home working. They are a truly mobile office person and the traditional 9–5 business atmosphere just does not equate to this group.

An example:

An agent was chastised by his manager for not playing well in the "sandbox". The agent was new to the office, a Gen X guy, who worked from his laptop everywhere he could, most often at home or at the nearby Starbucks, hated attending long boring unfocused, poorly presented sales meeting that were best described as not at all inspirational. He had a transaction a month and was creating solid revenue for the office, yet the office team saw this person as a loner, not interested in playing with the team and truly only focused on his own business issues. He was rarely in the office building relationships with the team and they saw him as distant and not a part of the group. They were also jealous of his tech skills, which had him working in a different style than they were used to. The reality was, however, he was truly productive, but, because he was not working in the model the Generational groups were used to seeing, they chastised him as a slacker who did not play by their rules.

Yet were the rules even appropraite for productive business in today's business model for that agents peer group needs?

- So I told my boss, "If you are looking for loyalty, buy a dog."

By and large, Generation Xers are seeking portable, transferable careers and solid résumé growth. They will remain with an organization as long as they believe they benefit from staying. As soon as they sense instability, or perceive a better growth opportunity elsewhere, they move quickly. They saw what happened to previous generations who devoted their lives to a single organization, and that memory taints their sense of workplace loyalty.

The Traditionalist is the most loyal in most real estate organizations. The thought of moving to another environment puts them behind the curve. The Boomer needs the connection of its peer group for strength and comfort. The Gen X person does not seek loyalty at all, they seek experiences. They have seen the loyalty their parents gave to jobs blow up in their faces and have a cynical approach to what a future based upon loyalty can look like. The Gen x group will only remain in an organization when they feel that the growth is tangible, when the experiences are focused and developmental and when leadership is clearly focused on a strategic business purpose.

An example:

Leigh was an agent with enthusiasm that joined an office. Upon joining the manager chose a mentor for his progress and charged Leigh half of every commission earned to compensate the mentor. This was on top of being at a 50/50 split to start. As business developed the manager would not reverse her policy that every agent needed a mentor, and in fact was not truly available to Leigh. In addition Leigh had done a great deal of business for a new agent, but at the same time over a number of months, had some real disappointments with transactions that fell through.

The agent called and emailed his manager continually for a meeting. Her response was she only had time for agents who were doing business. The reality was he had written $3,000,000 in contracts in 60 days, all of which fell apart. He suddenly left the office and the manager could not believe that with all she had done for him this was where it ended up. The manger could not believe the lack of loyalty .

- "A hiring bonus? You are too wet behind the ears for a hiring bonus!"

Remember, Generation Xers were reared in the age of performance-based stock options. Many became wealthy off the options they chose. Although that bubble has burst, Xers still believe that the bonus is a trade off for wages.

The Gen X person is looking for future benefits.

- "I have a new rule—no meetings after 5:00 p.m. I have a life."

The Xer group does not see real value in structured meetings. They prefer teleconference, email, and nontraditional meeting formats. They truly crave personal time as they have seen their parents sacrifice too much only to be down sized. They are not willing to work for their career at all costs.

An example:

Business had not been easy so the manager of an office decided to have two call nights where agents would come in a as a group activity call into an area to get listing appointments. The Gen X agent thought this a ridiculous waste of time. His prospecting style was different and taking a night away form his young family just did not equate. He thought that was just a silly way to organize a team to get business.

- "She wants a career map? How do I know?"

The Gen Xer is looking for the line of travel; if I do this here, will that get me there? They are looking for a feature/benefit career path, and they want to see a strategy to the journey they are taking. Unlike Traditionalists, they do not believe in paying dues. They want the focus to be on where they will go, how they will get there, and what tasks are valuable so they can reach their next station in career building.

An example:

Darcy has been a manager in another industry for year's when she decided to sell real estate. As a Gen X person she has asked her manger for guidance and insight about what her future might look like in the organization. The manger was not aware of how to deal with this. Darcy was frustrated as she did not have a focus for her long range career goals. The lack of organizational direction for a career path frustrates her and she is now seeking other company options where someone can help her create a learning strategy.

- "If I hear we tried that in 87 one more time…"

The Xer is not at all history focused. They want to know they can bring new ideas and make a contribution to the organization. A focus on history that might inspire previous generations is an instant turn off to the Xer.

An example

Business has become difficult. The manager does not have recent recall of when the last time business was in the condition that it is now, the last time being the Real Estate market was in 1990. Business was done differently then, and the technology of today didn't exist then. In fact the AOL had only been in existence a year.

At an office meeting the manager suggested that the agents all walk a neighborhood and door knock. That was what she recalled worked in 1990.

The four Gen X agents that work in the office were floored by the lack of modern ingenuity to create business. When they asked their manager how they might all use the internet to create business leads, she was clueless. They were frustrated that the mangers business guidance reference point was a 16 year old strategy that may not even work.

Other conflict zones that tend to surface persistently are perceptions over status quo, reward for tenure, and styles of training.

For thirty years, Boomers and Traditionalists held a tug of war over the status quo, with Boomers challenging it relentlessly and Traditionalists struggling to maintain it. The coveted corner offices were highly prized and not easily won.

Traditionalists, long term reward seekers, believe you need to pay your dues to earn your position in the company, while Generation Xers believe reward should be based on productivity, not tenure.

In terms of training, Traditionalists learned the hard way (through the school of hard knocks) and they feel others should too. Boomers believe time spent training in non-productive related concepts opens the door for people to go elsewhere. But for the Xer and Millennial, training is key to retention.

Conflict zones are common areas for generational clashes to occur. Each generation has its own unique way of responding to workplace behaviors and interactions. What one generation embraces, another finds offensive. It's important to recognize conflict zones to alleviate what often becomes the target of workplace complaints and grievances. Recognize conflict zones before they affect morale, performance, and productivity and turn the generation gap into generation knowledge.

Think About It...

- What challenges are you seeing in your work environment among the four generations?

- What dialogues do you hear that reflect potential conflict zones?

GENERATIONAL PERCEPTIONS

How Others View Boomers

Traditionalists think of Boomers	Gen Xers think of Boomers
They are self-absorbed	They are self-righteous
They are resentful of older leadership	They are workaholics
They talk about things they shouldn't	They are too political
	They are into the fad of the week

How Others View Xers

Traditionalists think of Gen Xers	Boomers think of Gen Xers
They don't know enough	They are slackers
They don't respect experience	They are rude and lack social skills
They don't follow the rules	They want to do everything their way
They don't know what hard work is	They think the internet solves everything
They are too quick to change jobs	They are impatient

RECRUITING THE FOUR GENERATIONS

Attracting multi-generation talent to your organization means knowing who your candidates are and what they are looking for.

The Traditionalist candidate is willing to be sold, the boomer candidate wants to convince you they are a great candidate, the Gen Xer is looking for your unique business solutions, the Millennial is looking for acceptance.

Often today's candidates, most notably the Gen X and the Millennial, are confident and tech savvy with high expectations and zero tolerance for mediocrity. Before they walk through your door, they've done their research. If the recruiting messages do not speak to their specific goals, they will find someplace else that will. The Boomer and Traditionalist are less focused on the outside view looking relying more on emotion then facts.

While income and stability used to be the primary factors determining job selection, candidates today place a greater value on a myriad of other benefits such as flexibility and rapid growth opportunities. If you don't understand what your candidates want, your attempt to target your message is random at best and ineffective at worst.

When you understand the goals of your candidate, you can highlight the value of your benefits. Most candidates today want a flexible schedule that allows for balance between home and work, but the reason each generation wants that flexibility is unique.

Traditionalists, having spent a lifetime working, want to enjoy time with grandchildren and still have the opportunity for travel and personal growth. Boomers, at a point of change and transition in their lives, want flexibility as they to juggle the needs of aging parents while supporting kids in college and at home. Generation Xers, not willing to wait until retirement to enjoy friends and family, want a schedule that allows them to stay involved in their children's lives. They also seek true business recipes that are brand recognizable. Millennials, who grew up darting from one activity to another, are not ready to give up the freedom of a schedule rich with non-work-related activities.

Understanding the unique desires of each generation enables you to articulate value proposition and reposition benefits to match the aspirations of your candidate. How you position those messages for each candidate will determine the success of your recruiting efforts?

In the Real estate industry the traditionalist thinking always allowed the agent to pick and choose from brand tools without requirement. The brand itself was a nice tool but not a real asset in the life of the typical traditionalist agent. The power of the brand was always optional. No longer is that acceptable business strategy.

The mind set has always been that leadership in the industry cannot tell an agent how to work and the Traditionalist and Boomer always accepted this. The Gen X person, however, truly wants focused tool direction. What tools are the ones that work best and how can they re-invent them?

Look in the Right Place

Finding the right people means looking in the right place. Newspaper classifieds might work well for Traditionalists and Boomers, but Xers and Millennials are searching for you digitally.

Candidates in this age group look to the global community for information about your organization. They check Craigslist and Monster.com, and look to blogs and chat rooms to generate a real life picture of your organization. They have already explored your website and judged you on its progressive features, its ability to access information, and whether it has images representative of a diverse employee population.

Interviewing: Seek To Understand, Then To Be Understood

The most common mistake interviewers make is to do too much talking and not enough listening. Interviewers fail to position the relevant messages because they do not take the time to assess the goals of the candidates and their career paths. Dialogues tend to focus on the past instead of the future, and they too often fixate on the organization rather than the individual. Interviewers with an understanding of generational differences can highlight the benefits and features that appeal to your population. Without this understanding, true rapport is rarely established, and an honest interview is hard to obtain.

Understanding Traditionalists

The greatest asset Traditionalists bring to the workforce is their years of experience. Respect and appreciate their hard won experience, and dote on their accomplishments as they have truly paid their dues to achieve long-term results. When interviewing Traditionalists, they recognize that their respect for authority will often hinder their ability to talk freely. Open-ended, future-focused questions will help to create the rapport they need for a frank discussion.

Traditionalists often return to the workplace after a stint of retirement. They want to continue leading active, meaningful lives but with a new twist of freedom. After so many years in the workforce, they expect flexible schedules so they can enjoy a balance between family, recreation, and work.

The traditionalist candidate will sit and listen—in fact, they prefer a manager that presents, and tries to sell rather than be engaged in a dialogue where they as a candidate need to respond.

This is a tremendously respectful group—they will listen attentively and would prefer not to share much about themselves. They will have done very little research in advance and will seek out a place they will be comfortable.

Understanding Boomers

Political Boomers are continuously positioning during their interview as they strive to appear polished and professional. Their primary concern is to be hired; only later will they analyze the particulars of the organization. They are reticent, tending to keep their conversations vague and general as they scope the scene. They are buzzword and sound bite focused as this makes them feel very "cool." When they're comfortable, they'll lay their credentials on the table. Throughout the interview strive to move past their cautiousness to understand their goals and values.

Boomers are excellent team players, however, a competitive spirit underscores their individualism. They view themselves as stars of their own show. Focus on this "star" mentality as you praise their unique accomplishments to emphasize the value they bring to your organization.

Boomers bring terrific assets to the work environment. Their consumerism gives them an appreciation for quality services, and with this understanding they strive to be service oriented in their own practices. They have high expectations for their performance and are driven to go the extra mile to deliver a job well done.

This group truly wants to be hired in the interview process. They are tuned in (at least in their non minds) and will use sound bytes they have heard to build interviewer confidence that they are, indeed, suitable candidates. They will exude a decision mode posturing to get hired. They do not seek details, they will gloss over the issues to try and reach out to get a quick resolution. They will respond to lots of generalities of potential success and do not need or seek details.

Understanding Generation X

Generation X grew up in the wake of corporate reshuffling and failed companies. They saw the burst of the dot.com bubble and with it the disappearance of lifetime retirement dreams. Their skepticism for an organization's longevity is palpable and their goals reflect that skepticism. Futurists predict Generation Xers will work for an average of seven different companies in their lifetime. They are the hardest segment to retain, as their desire for freedom and potentially brighter horizons keep them from staying in any one organization for too long.

Generation Xers' career goal is to maintain balance and autonomy, and this means developing their skills so that no matter where they go, they will be employable. They want opportunities for acquiring an extended skill base and an enhanced portfolio that will guarantee their employability should some sort of emergency occur. The more you can promote their self-growth, the greater your chance of retaining Xers.

Unlike Traditionalists and Boomers who live to work, Generation Xers work to live. They were raised by parents who put work first, and as a consequence they seek balance in their own lives.

Offer a real life perspective of what it is like to work for your organization. Talk about peers who have achieved rapid success using your business model so Xers can envision themselves in your environment. Create vivid differentiation by demonstrating how your unique tools and cutting edge technology increase productivity.

This candidate will have done a ton of researching, from blogs and chat rooms about the organization to searching the internet to find every possible piece of information that they can to help guide their decision.

Understanding Millennials

While Millennials are the smallest segment of our industry at this time, we will soon find ourselves turning to them to fill the managerial gap left by retiring Traditionalists and Boomers. Organizations will have to target their messages and create compelling packages to compete for the most talented Millennials to fill the void that is too great for Gen Xers to satisfy.

Despite their lack of experience, Millennials want to be treated like colleagues not kids. They want to see a work environment that is upbeat and optimistic, dynamic and creative, and culturally diverse. They also want fun, informal work environments and flexible, non-conventional work schedules so they can maintain their outside interests.

The Millennial's goal is to build a parallel career that will extend their marketability. Futurists predict Millennials will hold an average of ten different careers in their lifetime. They will not tolerate stagnation. If they do not feel as though they are continuously growing and learning, they will move on.

Because Millennials grew up volunteering and performing community service, they want organizations who work for a greater good and who contribute to the communities they serve. Accustomed to working in teams throughout their school years, Millennials prefer social and collaborative work environments. They grew up as active participants in the decisions that guided their life, and therefore expect access to leadership and inclusion in important workplace decisions.

Millennials never knew life without technology. Cutting edge technology with dynamic tools and resources are essential.

ASSETS AND LIABILITIES OF BOOMERS AND GENERATION XERS

Boomers on the Job

Assets	Liabilities
Service oriented	Not budget minded
Driven	Uncomfortable with conflict
Willing to go the extra mile	Reluctant to go against peers
Want to please	Tend to put process before results
Team Players	Judgmental
Competitive	Self-centered

Generation Xers on the Job

Assets	Liabilities
adaptable	impatient
technologically savvy	poor people skills
independent	cynical
unintimidated by authority	inexperienced
creative	unseasoned

ARTICULATING YOUR VALUE PROPOSITION AND REPOSITIONING BENEFITS

Lancaster and Stillman, in their book *When Generations Collide*, define a value proposition as, "A persuasive argument of what you have to offer aimed at appealing to a particular generation of recruits that is focused on the audience, not on the organization." In other words, it's the "What's in it for me?" message that your candidate listens for during the interview process.

Candidates today look for specific value and benefits such as flexible schedules, cutting-edge technology, inspiring work environments, and opportunities for growth and skill development. If you don't understand what your candidates want, you cannot hope to frame the value proposition to meet their goals. When you understand their goals, you can communicate those benefits to each generation. It's important to realize that no matter how stellar your value proposition, it's meaningless if recruiters and interviewers don't masterfully communicate it.

Traditional value messages that appealed to previous generations are often ineffective when presented to Generation X. Skeptical Xers have hawk-like senses when it comes to spotting a phony value proposition. Reposition benefits to accommodate what you know of your candidates, and they will listen. When you praise the size of your organization, Xers hear "bureaucracy." Reposition size with the myriad of opportunities your working environment offers. When you focus on your organization's history and tradition, Xers hear "resistant to change." Reposition history with a drive for constant growth and a reinvention of business strategy. When you applaud your availability 24/7, Xers think—get a life. Clarify accessibility with specifics: "I'm available via e-mail or Blackberry 24/7." What you say and how you say it depends on whom you are saying it to.

Value propositions inspire and excite. They are energetic and optimistic. They highlight innovation, new business dynamics, fast paced learning, coaching, and the ability to impact how business is done. Value messages address the diversity of the workforce, while sharing commonalities among generations. Most of all, value propositions keep front and center the answer to the question, "Why would these generations want to work for me?"

Value Package Statements to re-evaluate and how they fall flat on a Gen x person

"We have 1500 offices......"

This is an industry cliché where we use organizational size to justify the reason to affiliate. In fact the boutique group has always used the anti size as their ability to recruit. Size may be a relevant message for a traditionalist and a boomer as they rely upon the security of large institutions as a valuable asset. The large venerable company is an empty message to Gen X person. They do not connect to the reputations of market leadership. They have seen many "well reputed' companies fail. The failures of major brands add to the cynicism that Gen X people carries forward. They do not trust the size of organizations to be an asset. They see a worldwide community and a limited number of offices, no matter what the size of the organization, it does not re-enforce their perception of a global business world. Size alone is not an asset to Gen X person—multiple market opportunities is.

"We have great tools……"

Every organization boasts the tools the have to enable an agent to do business. The challenge is every organization essentially has similar tools. The tools must reflect strategy for Gen X person that represents a unique business model brand focused tools that differentiate this brand form another. The positioning of business tools cannot emulate another brand. Clarity of advantage is a real factor for a Gen X. Their natural cynicism creates suspicion about the use of their tools and it seems unclear why this brand is a choice.

The focus requirement of what tools need to be used is vital for the Gen X person. They will strive to re-invent but need the tools so they can re-invent effectively. Coaching and ability to re-invent business is a very important communication strategy instead.

"Our history in the market place is outstanding"

This is a typical interviewer comment about their company. It is a non-issue for a Gen X person. This, again, relates to the cynicism they feel about organization that no longer exist or have any value to them, but were trusted leadership models in the past. Many organizations that had big brand impact are no longer important. To an Gen X person new brands emerge all of the time that create niche markets negating the value of brands that may have been trusted in the past. Where was Google just five years ago? The brands that were trusted historically such as Xerox, for example have been replaced by newer more inventive brands. The length of time doing business is not necessarily an asset.

New business strategy and re-invented systems, which differentiate this organizations business recipe from another's, are the critical communication process. The solution here is not the history but rather the business solutions that are current.

"Our market share is dominant"

Although this is a statement that makes Traditionalists and Gen Xers feel good it is not a statement that motivates a Gen X agent. Most companies that boast their market share are often relics and war horses in the industry that are not necessarily creating new and exciting business models. Look at GM, once the leaders in the US auto industry is now a joke to Gen X person. Most have never even bought an American car. Many companies present market share as a positioning strategy, but to the top Gen X person this is not a truly valuable message. Apple is not the biggest computer company but yet this company totally markets itself toward the Gen X consumer. The Gen X candidate looks for ways to reach their peer group buyers, and cares more about that then they do market share. New and emerging business models need to be discussed as it relates to achieving business. Not how many consumers use the services. The Gen X'er looks for business relevance in their generational goals.

Think About It...

• What are the non-valuable, trusted messages Traditionalists and Boomers position to Xers and Millennials?

• How are we presenting our passion for our proprietary business model?

• How do we present the tools of our business so that each generation connects to them?

• Which messages are critical to share and which should we omit?

• Which messages will create clashes and vacuums of understanding?

Orienting, Training, and Managing the Four Generations: Success From the Start

Orienting

One of the unique challenges in the multi-generational arena is how we orient. The tone you set from day one is the tone that will linger. If you want excitement to reverberate throughout your office, create it from the start with a compelling and engaging program targeted to the diversity of your population. Outstanding orienting programs offer multiple modalities to enrich your presentation and address the learning styles of your affiliates. Don't linger on drawn-out descriptions of your organization's history or the ancillary services you provide unless those descriptions are directly tied to how they impact personal growth. Teach what your affiliates need most, such as business strategy and how to ensure productivity, but honor the generational differences represented in your audience. A dynamic orienting program presents the recipe for success for every individual while defining your expectations and motivating your agents the moment they walk through the door.

Orienting Traditionalists:

- Focus on why this segment of your population is important to the organization

- Talk about how they can get beyond feeling behind the times

- Encourage conversation with an understanding that respect for authority may inhibit their openness

Orienting Boomers:

- Recognize that Boomers are accustomed to plunging in headfirst

- Focus on the evolution of the company and how that evolution impacts current business practices

- Create a clear picture of their place within the strategy and direction of your organization

- Offer frequent opportunities to interact with leadership rather than long hours in a classroom

Orienting Xers:

- Recognize their goal is to gain experience for career growth

- Present cutting edge workplace advantages

- Demonstrate accessibility to information through intranet and other tools

- Make training interactive

- Map out career path

Orienting Millennials:

- Clarify strategy for accessing work related processes

- Explain processes with a focus on the "why"

- Make training highly interactive, hands-on, and fast-paced

- Engage, don't lecture

TRAINING

The world is changing faster than at any other time in history. Each new business trend creates a need for coordinated training with multi-level options for everyone within the organization. The one size fits all approach to training is no longer effective for the diversity of the workplace. Progressive training programs are like retention insurance; programs that cater to the goals of your agents and their success within your organization, strengthen their ties to your company.

Training does not have to be limited to a classroom setting with a primary facilitator. Generation Xers and Millennials appreciate options that include self-guided, on-line programs, as long as those programs offer opportunities for follow-up and feedback.

When you opt for a traditional training environment, remember the little things make the biggest impact. Comfort is key; nothing will negate the benefits of learning faster than hard chairs, poor lighting, long hours, and small print that strains the eyes. Snacks and drinks take little effort but go a long way in helping to keep your audience satisfied and alert.

Shake up training with stimulating activities, varying formats, and opportunities for interaction among participants. Training sessions are often one of the few occasions affiliates have to connect with one another. Take advantage of the diversity of your workforce and capitalize on the experiences of your audience to offer a dynamic and engaging environment. Each generation brings its own set of challenges and learning preferences to the training environment. Recognize your multi-generational audience and use your understanding of generational differences to create training that is inspiring and productive.

Traditionalists

Traditionalists grew up learning from the school of hard knocks, with time and experience as their teachers. They prefer to listen and learn in a passive, lecture-style format. They will not challenge the trainer or participate in discussions unless they are strongly encouraged to open up. Introduce new concepts in bite size pieces and focus on short-term results.

An example:

Sally was going to training. She was thrilled that her first activities in the office were going to revolve around training. She had to wait for the "fast start' program to start which was a month after her affiliation. Her manager gave her busy work to accom-

plish, but none of these task edged Sally toward her first piece of business. Sally was in fact relieved to be given time to find her way. Sally was a typical Traditionalist agent, wanting to learn lots of information so she can feel she has the answers to questions before she jumps in. Not having all of the answers in advance makes her very nervous and as a result keeps her from feeling secure. By not having to jump in she has comfort and knows that one day, after she has really learned everything, she will feel ready.

Boomers

Boomers harbor a gatekeeper approach to information. They believe if you spend too much time training, agents will take what they've learned and go somewhere else. Boomers favor a fact-based, Cliff Notes version of training, and they prefer mixed media presentations to straight lectures. They require constant feedback and reinforcement to feel positive about their progress.

An Example:

Alan is a boomer agent new to an office. He has been looking at the Real Estate industry recently as he is retiring and wants to continue to work. He has a certain tech skill level and is looking to get some quick information so he can get started. Alan really hates details and wants to jump in and cross the "i's" and dot the "t's" later. He is confident as he has always jumped in feet first and feels he can handle anything.

He is not into getting materials ready and he is not willing to do the research he needs to do to get going. He feels he can wing it pretty successfully if someone pointed which direction to go in. In fact he assumes he can make it happen just because of his accumulated experiences and the success he has seen from so many of his peers in the industry.

His challenge is he is not willing to sit and listen to long lectures on how to do business. He wants the big bullet points, but feels he is being held back. Details just bore him to tears.

After a month in the office he had received a listing and wrote a contract. His manager did not recognize this achievement, as he is not yet a top producer. In fact, he had not even had a meeting with his manager since orientation was finished. His mentor worked the deal with him. This was the way the manager ran the office. New people are assumed to be a time eating bunch so she delegated it to a group of mentors. The manager who was too busy with other agent activities did not even know the listing and sale took place for a week until the manager was updated by the mentor.

Alan felt listless in his progress as the manager was not tuned into his recent success. He was considering other options but his friends worked in the office so he was thinking he would stick it out. Being a loner in an environment without people he knew was a concern to him, and he wrestled with the idea of staying on in a place he was just not appreciated.

He wanted the attention of a personalized touch form his manager.

Generation Xers

For Generation X, the more they learn the longer they'll stay. They equate training with growth and growth with stability. Being the skeptics that they are, they want to know the credentials of their trainer. Xers will feel they have plateaued with your organization if training opportunities end. Generation Xers prefer training that incorporates problem solving and real-life case studies. A flat, monotone presentation with dated tools (like overheads) will instantly disengage your Xer audience. They want interactive presentations using multiple media formats and new methodologies with continuous retooling.

An example:

Brett is a new Gen X agent that has just joined the office. He is eager to get started and based upon his "craigslist" post has generated several recent leads this weekend. He was told by his manager that he needed to wait for fast start to learn all about the things he needs to know but that is four weeks away.

He wanted to get started immediately and wanted to avail himself of on-line learning resources, but his manager was not familiar with the details of those tools and was not confident that they would satisfy the learning needs that were required.

In fact as he questioned his manager about the delay, she frankly stated this was the way training was handled. The online options could not possibly be a substitute for the classroom.

He was determined to seek out the resources he needed, and was anxious to find the brand tools that would enable his business. The challenge was there was no true formula appearing process that he could take advantage of.

He started seeking training blogs, and the company did not have any—nor were there FAQ's to guide him.

When he discussed this with his manager she was just to overwhelmed and not used to such needs to have a focused tangible response.

Millennials

Millennials view training in a very different light than the generations before them. They are comfortable with continuously changing technology and the rapid flow of information. Because of this, they see training as a lifelong process rather than a final product of attainment. They want engaging training environments that are structured yet fun. Experiential learning, with opportunities for teamwork and multi-tasking, match the Millennial learning style.

MANAGING AND GIVING FEEDBACK: DEVELOPING A COACHING CULTURE

Management sets the tone for harmony in the office. The presence of multiple generations, each with their own view of the world and their own patterns of behavior, create a challenge for any organization. Perceptions of fairness and equality influence morale, productivity, and ultimately retention. As the work environment grows in complexity, managers must conscientiously strive to understand the diverse dispositions of their affiliates. Businesses that fail to address generational diversity will watch as the most talented people walk out the door. When you embrace the multiplicity of experience available in your office, and create a coaching culture that addresses the unique needs of your population, attracting and retaining the most talented people will occur naturally.

Each generation has its own style of interacting with management. It is management's responsibility to appreciate the differences, recognize shortcomings, and develop feedback that is sensitive to the needs of your affiliates.

Traditionalists

- Traditionalists notoriously maintain the status quo and are therefore hesitant to accept new business models. They have a deep aversion for anything that threatens to replace long held business practices.

- The idea of having to be open, frank, and candid are not traits that Traditionalists typically share. They prefer to hide behind silence and not rock the boat.

- Traditionalists prefer the familiarity of top-down management styles. As a top down style creates comfort, they are not willing to go out on a limb to offer opinions.

- In coaching, they fear not knowing an answer and as a result fear being vulnerable to failure.

- Traditionalists will patiently seek long-term rewards.

Feedback Styles: Traditionalists prefer communication that is face-to-face or written. When giving feedback, use formal language and don't expect a solicitous response. They do not require continuous feedback or stroking, and in fact, view it as invasive. As far as they're concerned, no news is good news.

An example

Marjorie had been an agent in the office for many years. She was a solid agent never really getting her business above a certain level. Her manager had suggested that there might be value in a weekly coaching session.

Marjorie was not sure how this would work. After all why do something different. It might make her feel awkward to need to talk weekly about her business. She had never done that before. She was comfortable thinking that nothing was really wrong with her business although in the big picture she would like to increase her unit flow. The idea of reporting in weekly was not quite a true need for her. In fact she was not sure the idea of talking openly about her business "failings" was something she wished to do.

Why did she need to do this anyway?

Boomers

- While Traditionalists clung to the status quo, Boomers spent the past thirty years fighting to challenge it. Boomers' anti-establishment nature successfully challenged the chain of command and traditional organization structures.

- They have a love/hate relationship with authority. They will not usually challenge decisions made by management, but they require a great deal of explanation.

- Boomers like to be recognized for the value they bring to the organization. Focus on how important this group is to the business and emphasize the unique accomplishments they bring.

Feedback Styles: Boomers prefer face-to-face feedback with open, direct dialogue. They thrive on positive feedback as the political nature of negative feedback is unnerving to them; they worry about who might hear. They expect formal feedback to come once or twice a year with lots of documentation. They like continuous reinforcement and stroking from management to affirm the path they are on.

An Example:

Gary was a real needy, good news focused agent. He loved hearing from leadership when things were going well and he loved getting monthly rewards and recognition. However he too was invited to join in a coaching program. This was fine with him, but the conversation went towards area of development and the details he would need to advance his business.

He felt truly uncomfortable as he had only heard good news in the past and was wondering if the feedback he was receiving was truly valid. As he had never had this sort of feedback before, he was totally ignoring it and not looking to see it as valuable.

Generation Xers

- Generation Xers are unaffected by status quo.

- They have no tolerance for dated technology or lengthy wait times when they are trying to attain information.

- Unproductive meetings and obligatory social gatherings that pretend to be work related are agonizing for them. They prefer teleconferencing, e-mail, and non-traditional meeting formats that don't infringe on their personal time.

- Xers expect direct and clear paths to decision making. Complex and challenging routes to answers will turn them off immediately.

- They want to be rewarded for their performance, not their tenure.

- This group wants to know that leadership is coaching their success. Leadership must set the tone to achieve, converse often about the achievements, and allow Xers to reinvent solutions.

- Xers expect to be accountable for results. They will get their work done with creativity and resourcefulness, but to the beat of their own clock. They prefer to do much of their work at home and meet with their clients at Starbucks. As soon as they feel micro-managed, they run.

Feedback Styles: While Generation Xers resent infringements on their time for meetings and events they deem unnecessary, time spent on feedback is essential. Xers crave feedback. Conversations with Xers must be meaningful and productive. This was the generation that viewed the show *Friends* as a role model and found that relaxed communication was just fine.

They are not afraid to ask how they are doing, and will regularly share information informally. In fact, they crave resources such as FAQs to get their answers rather than the face-to-face meetings many have been used to in the past. IMs are a critical feedback style for this group.

An example

Laurel has been in the office for some time and is insisting on twice weekly meetings with her manager to discuss business progress. The Traditionalist manager finds this a true intrusion on time that she could spend with other: whether handling transactional issues or other tasks. Laurel wants to discuss the business issues at hand on a weekly basis and is seeking input to use new untried business models. She is really frustrated that the manager will not present meeting agendas and updates on the office website, and finds the managers lack of driven interest in her business frustrating. She wants to be rewarded for her achievements by being led to new career options and additional company led training. The manager is not prepared to have that level of discussion as she is not even clear what direction to give. The Manager likes Laurel and wishes she would be content just dong business, but Laurel wants more. She seeks to be directed to strategies that can help her do business more efficiently than her boomer/traditionalist peers seem to accept and wants to push ahead creating new business options and reach her peers ion a new business approach. The manager reluctantly commits to a once a month meeting time, but feels this is even excessive.

Millennials

- Millennials expect flexibility, informality, fun, and camaraderie. They want structure with room for creativity.

- Cutting edge technology and progressive tools are essential.

- Millennials want managers who don't take themselves too seriously and who are not afraid to show a sense of humor.

- They want to be involved in the decision-making processes that affect their work life. When they understand and agree with your rules, they will follow them loyally.

Feedback Styles: Millennials expect systematic, frequent, now-time feedback. They were raised on rubrics and constructive criticism and will interpret silence as a sign of disapproval. They prefer to communicate using e-mail and voicemail.

An example:

Shezan is a new millennial agent. Her battle to learn is complicated by the fact everyone in her environment looks at a 25 year old agent and almost with disdain can not comprehend how she can even consider doing business. She is constantly wired to her IM group and wants to daily meet with her traditionalist manager to talk about activities that will be of benefit that day.

The traditionalist Manager seems to think Shezan is in a tremendous hurry, and works hard to slow her pace down. It makes no sense to her that an agent should expect daily interaction, especially before she goes to fast start.

Once fast start happens two full days are spent in lecture about how to use basic technology. Shezan asks why this is such a big deal as the class group has seemingly never used email an is learning how for the first time. This is a frustration and while she is in class is wirelessly surfing the net looking for training solutions on line. While in class she went to "myspace" and found that she has resources there to get leads. Through her blog, she has been conversing with two potential buyers, and has no interest in the dull lecture she is attending.

She also has allowed herself to be photographed for the new office bill board. She is tiny and has a very petite frame. Somehow in the picture taking she looks quite well endowed and as if her head was placed on a different body. Everyone teased her to the point that she put in her blog "if you buy a house from me I'll show you my t-ts".

Her manager who had little interest before, suddenly took interest in a different way, and threw Shezan out of the office.

Caveats for Managing the Generations

Mentoring and coaching should be an integral part of every organizational plan. Performance is only enhanced when the diverse perspectives and experience of a multi-generational workforce is nurtured. Within this environment, maintain standards of expectations and clearly defined objectives.

1. Respect the experience that every generation brings, young and old.

2. Never talk down to anyone.

3. Model what you expect, and prove you are not above learning new strategies.

4. Don't pretend to know all the answers. Xers and Millennials, in particular, admire the honesty of an, *I don't know, but I'll look into it* answer.

5. Don't assume your way is the best way or the most favored way.

6. Respect the speed factor of each generation. Xers and Millennials often move at a pace difficult for Traditionalists and Boomers to maintain.

7. Make meetings and team building meaningful and result oriented.

8. Negative attitudes breed negativity.

9. Always give your affiliates the benefit of the doubt.

10. Be flexible.

11. Be Patient.

12. Don't assume.

13. Provide continuous feedback.

14. Seek to understand, then to be understood.

Think About It...

• Are we boring new affiliates with details about our ancillary services?

• Are we teaching business strategy?

• Are we lecturing or creating interactive, problem solving, learning environments?

• Are we presenting the recipe for career success?

• Are we creating excitement on the first day?

• How is our current orientation model failing each generation? What can be changed?

• Where are we having challenges giving relevant feedback to the teams we manage?

• Are we using a feedback loop in our coaching practices?

Retention: Preventing the Revolving Door from Becoming Unhinged—facing Retention Deficit Disorder

The economic effect of the revolving door that plagues our industry is both concrete and elusive. Time and money drain from organizations as resources devoted to recruiting and training disappear with each new swing of the door. When the most experienced and talented people leave for brighter horizons, the entire organization feels the loss. Relationships and contacts disappear, morale lowers, insecurities rise, and the recruiting cycle begins anew.

While Traditionalists and Boomers currently dominate our industry, their future retirement will leave a void that organizations will find themselves scrambling to fill. Generation X, significantly smaller in number than their predecessors, will be unable to satisfy the demand, and the industry will turn to young Millennials for leadership positions that they may be ill-prepared to take on.

When affiliates feel they don't belong they will leave, usually without any feedback as to why. Evaluate your affiliate's reasons for leaving to learn what you could have done differently.

Retention Factors for Traditionalists

Traditionalists are an easy group to retain. If you are losing this segment, check the barometer of your company, as there might be something wrong. When the loyal start to leave, there is a challenge. Exiting Traditionalists take with them a reservoir of experience and an extensive client base built over many years in the profession. For this group, job change is a stigma, and they generally leave an organization only as a last resort. When you lose Traditionalists, it's time to do some honest soul searching to find out why the most loyal and devoted segment of the population is stepping down.

An example:

Barry was a seasoned long-term manager of several years. He played golf three days a week and was certainly well aware of the office needs. He prospected for business and fed it to his agents on a regular basis. He took his agents business needs very seriously, and when he was out of the office always looked for business to get him going.

Barry took care of his traditionalist agents in trouble. One day John came in, truly angst ridden about something and to cheer him up gave him two listing leads.

Another agent, Lester came in the next day and was in a bad mood over a transaction falling apart. Barry gave him a lead. The next day Joan, another traditionalist agent, came in having lost out on a listing presentation. Barry gave her two buyer leads.

Phyllis, another traditionalist agent, never went to Barry for anything or complained. As a result she never received a lead

This group, plus another, all ended up in a deli for lunch. As they were talking Barry came up in conversation. After listening to the group it was determined how unfair Barry was. No one could believe that if you have a bad day and go complain, Barry hands out free business. The group was so shocked at Barry's behavior that they all left the office for a place that had rules of engagement.

Retention Factors for Boomers

The most common exit factor for Boomers is the lack of high profile options available to them. They are status oriented and symbol conscious, and they want to see opportunities to reach their high potential. Boomers view leaving as a negative that puts them behind the curve. They build strong relationships with their organizations and feel personally guilty when they break those ties.

An example:

Mona had been in the office for years. She worked there with a group of people that she knew well and also had been a close friend of the original office manager. She knew everyone in the Marketing Dept., the training dept., and in Accounting. If something went astray she knew who to call.

Recently the company was sold. Three of her friends were considering a move to a newer office (a competitor nearby). Her contact in accounting had retired, and her first commission check this month was wrong. No one knew who she was or who she should talk to, to fix it.

She also had a marketing challenge. She was looking to place several ads to promote herself, yet the marketing person she knew was now relocated to another division and the remaining staff could not see her for two weeks.

Her friends were all feeling the same pressure, the group went to interview elsewhere and left as they felt they no longer had a sphere of interest in the organization.

Retention Factors for Generation Xers

The most common exit factor for Xers is a sense of the organization's instability and a lack of skill development to enhance their career growth. When Generation Xers leave, it is purely a business move. Career hopping is a way of life for this segment of the population. Job change is a strategic imperative. They want skills that motivate them to stay and they want coached autonomy. Generation Xers will not stay in an organization that infringes on the balance they strive to maintain in their personal life. Commission structures can't buy them out at the expense of this balance. Your understanding of their career goals and the balance they seek, and the differentiation you offer to support their success, is critical to bucking the trend.

An Example:

Lisa has been in an office for 14 months. She has a boomer manager who has been happy to have her. Yet Lisa wants to learn how to develop business leads through several "e" business models. Her manager does not have a clue about how to guide her. The result is she leaves now joining her third office in three years. No one knows how to really coach her business.

Retention Factors for Millennials

For Millennials, job change is a way of life. Millennials want to see the opportunity for rapid progression and growth within the company. Their sense of time is such that what may seem like normal going through the ranks to other generations, will appear to be stagnation to Millennials. Key to retaining this group is options for multitasking and progressive training opportunities. Coaching, continuous feedback, and access to management are necessary for this group's retention.

An example:

Marla is 24. She has just graduated from college and thinks Real Estate is a valid career option for her. She has a "dreamy" sense of what this should look like and as a result has no ideas at all of how to get started. She seems so unanchored, although truly willing to do whatever it takes.

No one hires her because she seems so ill prepared; yet no one tells her what they expect.

*　　　*　　　*　　　*

The psychology of retention is pivotal to preventing a loss of talent. Retention falls back on how we recruit. The revolving door turns far too often and far too early. Examine the turnover to find what is really causing it. Most of the time, it is a management related issue based on what is not being provided. Meaningful exit interviews are your most effective tool for analyzing the "whys" of leaving. Careful evaluations can offer a tremendous amount of information and discovery. The rifts you uncover open the door to creating practices that target your gaps and may serve to become your niche in the industry.

When you understand the challenges for each generation, you can recognize retention dilemmas. Now is the time to evaluate your recruiting practices. Who is being excluded and why? How does leadership adapt training practices for the diversity of your office? How do your affiliates receive your feedback? Step out of the security of your generational disposition to identify with the diversity around you. A talent war is brewing; organizations that don't target the four generations now, will find themselves prey to the whims of the revolving door.

Think About It…

- How can we use exit interviews in a meaningful manner?

- What keeps your affiliates from leaving?

- Why have certain affiliates left?

- How did you fail them, and how could you have achieved a different result?

In Conclusion:

Examine what you do well for each generation

Examine what needs to be shifted to appear valuable to each group

Actively assess the successes and failures offered to each generation as they are hired and as they produce

Assess how the brand is building generational success

Create strategies for growth based on generational needs

Make your brand tools valuable and linked to recipes for success—focus on the value

Reinforce the brand tools to build retention so that by losing the use of the tool each generation would feel the loss

Focus on messages to build retention

Focus on the generational need for career pathing and coaching for performance growth

Putting it all together...

So where do we go from here? Let's look at our four typical affiliates. The Traditionalist, struggled with feeling archaic and displaced. She felt challenged to change her time-honored methods of working with clients, and was threatened by the rapidly changing technology she was expected to use. Her practices had always worked in the past, as long as she persevered, but lately she wasn't as confident as she used to be. She was beginning to think of herself as a dying breed of agent and was second-guessing her ability to remain in the business at all.

The office managers, don't often recognize how to redirect agents to operate in a new way, but it have to be accessible and unintimidating. Understanding needs from a generational vantage point is a challenge.

Throughout the book there were examples of generational issues creating challenge.

Reviewing just four,

To be respected and acknowledged for experience, Jane focused on the benefits Mary's experience brought to the organization. She offered a traditional, lecture style training session where Mary could learn the value of the unique tools of the brand and was careful to offer training in small segments of routine installments so Mary could process the information and focus on short-term results. She put into place the training Mary needed, but conscientiously framed it around the value of Mary's years of experience. Jane consciously gave targeted, formal, face-to-face feedback that didn't require lengthy and gratuitous communication. With this approach, Mary was able to regain her former enthusiasm for her profession while gathering the skills she needed to compete with her colleagues. She regained the confidence to move forward, even at the last stages of her career.

Remember Sue, our ambitious Baby Boomer? Sue had enjoyed a career filled with public recognition and accolades. Now, with her company's new president, she felt undervalued and disassociated from the powers that be. Leadership's lack of acknowledgement toward her successes was beginning to diminish her motivation and was creating feelings of insecurity and isolation.

Jane's focus was to reenergize Sue to produce and thrive. Jane held a series of one-on-one sessions with Sue to give her a chance to feel connected to leadership and to paint a clear picture of her place within the organization. Recognizing her Boomer desire for recognition and feedback, Jane was direct and open with her communication. She offered lots of positive reinforcement and was careful to acknowledge and affirm Sue's many successes. Sue gradually began to feel more valued and involved and began, once again, to see herself as an essential, valued asset to the company.

Madison, our cynical, achievement oriented Generation Xer, was feeling stymied by the lack of progressive, independent training opportunities. She was not willing to sacrifice her time for traditional training sessions that moved at what she viewed as a snail's pace and that failed to speak to her specific goals. She was rapidly losing faith that her organization was even capable of defining its unique place in the industry.

Recognizing a Generation Xers pension for impatience, Jane knew if she didn't act quickly, Madison would be out the door. Madison needed cutting edge training and technology, and she needed it to be made available in a non-conventional setting and with a flexible schedule. She instituted a focused coaching program that addressed Madison's specific goals and she linked Madison to numerous training opportunities that would assure she would continue to acquire a new skill base in a variety of learning formats. Jane made herself available for productive, informal feedback, but more importantly, showed a respect for Madison's preference of communication by maintaining an open door via email and Instant Messaging.

As long as Jane continues to offer ongoing opportunities for growth through training and coaching, Madison will likely remain with the organization.

Finally, we'll return to Brittany, Jane's newest Millennial affiliate. Brittany's rich experience was technology based, rather than traditional career experience, and she felt frustrated and disillusioned at her organization's inability to value her for what she could offer. Jane's most pressing initiative was to carefully set a tone of respect and appreciation, independent of her affiliate's age and experience. This small, but significant gesture improved Brittany's morale and set the tone for an organization that focused on an affiliate's performance over her history.

When you look at what enabled Jane to meet the challenges of her multi-generational office both individually and holistically, you can easily see how knowledge and understanding drove her decisions and practices. When you understand your affiliate's world, you are empowered to create an organization that addresses everyone's needs, while sustaining your goal for continued growth and productivity. You now have the knowledge and tools to make a difference within your own organization and to turn the generational challenge into company wide success.

978-0-595-40129-1
0-595-40129-5

www.ingramcontent.com/pod-product-compliance
Lightning Source LLC
Chambersburg PA
CBHW021021180526
45163CB00005B/2050